Living in the Garden

God's Original Plan for Man
as told in GENESIS
Chapters 1 & 2

James N. "Chris" Harris, Jr.

ISBN: 978-0-578-77405-3
Copyright © 2020 by James N. Harris, Jr.
Publisher: James N. Harris, Jr.

Printed in the United States of America

Table of Contents

Preface

On the morning of November 5, 2012, I wrote in my journal, *Holy Spirit spoke to my heart and said that I should read, study, and develop intimacy with Genesis chapter 1 and 2, and see what I have in Christ Jesus...* That journey has brought me to a place of understanding, gratitude, thanksgiving, and appreciation of my Heavenly Father's love for me that brings me to tears. Writing *Living in the Garden* is my attempt to share with you what I have seen and come to understand over this journey.

My objective is that sharing what I have come to understand will challenge you to develop your own experience with our Heavenly Father. My experience will encourage you to look beyond the obvious and see into our Heavenly Father's heart and hear it beat, establishing the ultimate relationship.

During this journey, I quickly came to realize that these verses of scripture are the only record of God's relationship with man before there was sin, or separation of man from his Creator, and that they might help me understand God's intent for me, for our relationship, and for my purpose.

In my born-again experience I was never satisfied with the answers I had heard, and always desired to know more.

Understanding a little about me might help you understand the process I followed. I am a retired architect, the designer of buildings, creating environments, spaces, and systems that influence and facilitate human activity. The process that I followed as an architect was to first understand and then develop criteria that met a client's needs and objectives, environmental constraints, material and engineering considerations, and artistic considerations. This method caused me to develop a mindset of a step-by-step, well-considered process for life and the ability to design a solution that addresses, solves, and meets all project objectives.

So, when I accepted Jesus as Lord and Savior at 38 years of age, I followed a similar thought process in much of my Bible study. Some of my first areas of study were understanding God's plan for being a man, a husband, a father, the role of Holy Spirit in my life, and the like. I remember my study of being a father, and my responsibility to my children. I learned that it was my responsibility to learn all I could from God about life and then teach that to my children. I was always asking *why?* and *how?* And, just as designing a building, these studies would last weeks, or months, or even years, until there was a satisfactory conclusion.

This mindset has energized the last seven-plus years of study, meditation, and fellowship with

Holy Spirit to understand what Heavenly Father put into motion in Genesis, chapters 1 and 2.

- Why did He create me?
- What was my purpose?
- Why were the heavens and the earth created?
- What was His plan for all of this?
- What was His desired result?

Thank you for your desire to know more about His plan for our lives. I thank my HEAVENLY FATHER for His awesome love and goodness in this process.

Chapter One ~

The Principles

After reading Genesis, chapters 1 and 2, in several Bible translations numerous times in an effort to gain greater understanding, I began to meditate on the scriptures and ask Holy Spirit about the significance of what I was reading. After a period of time, I heard principles (meaning a fundamental truth or proposition that serves as the foundation for a system of belief or behavior or for a chain of reasoning) that helped me understand what I was reading. These principles served as my way of extracting truths from this time in Genesis 1 and 2. They are the foundation on which *Living in the Garden* was developed. This is what I heard and wrote in my journal. I invite you to read Genesis, chapters 1 and 2, first.

Genesis, Chapters 1 & 2
- *Principle One*

    The Spirit of God and the Word of God was involved in everything that God did.

Days later, after I had written out all the principles and had time to reflect on them, I heard God say to me; that if the Word of God and the Spirit of God is involved in everything that I do, it will all be perfect. What an awesome thought!

- *Principle Two*

    God said or spoke the things that He desired...and that was the only thing He ever said about that thing. Again, I heard in my spirit that if I only speak what I desire, things that are in harmony with God's Word, and nothing else, then I will always see that desired thing manifest.

- *Principle Three*

    God saw and inspected or evaluated what was produced from what He said and then declared it as "good." This labeling as "good" denotes His approval and acceptances and responsibility of what His words had produced. In Genesis 2:18, God says it is not good for man to be alone and then He makes a woman. God took responsibility for His words. And then I heard, "Do you take responsibility for your words; do you inspect and evaluate what your words produce? Words such as "I feel sick," or "I don't know how I will pay this bill," or "That tickles me to death."

- *Principle Four*

    God had an intelligent, considered, and well-conceived plan of what He desired... this is confirmed because He only said what He desired, and we can all testify that thousands of years later the wisdom of His creation is still unfolding. Again, I heard in my spirit, "Are your words intelligent, considered, well-conceived? Do you use your words to create what you desire, or do they create things that you do not want?"

- *Principle Five*

    God set a system of perpetual reproduction for all life...every living thing has within it the ability to reproduce itself...this includes His Word. God's Word is life, John 5:24, 6:63. Then I heard, "Do you use your words to produce good, so that they are continuously producing God's goodness in your life?"

- *Principle Six*

    God used this system of reproduction to perpetuate His creation of human beings, vegetation, animals, and all living things. His Word was the original seed that created a natural seed that perpetuated what He desired. Do you use your words to perpetuate good in your life?

- **Principle Seven**

   Everything that God made had a defined purpose and provision for its perpetual existence. Examine your words and understand the purpose behind them. Are they producing good or are you perpetuating evil with them?

- **Principle Eight**

   God judged everything that He did in Genesis, chapter 1 as "good" or "very good"; and then He rested. This position of rest denotes that His creation was equipped and empowered to fulfill His intended purpose without any further assistance from Him. This suggested His creation of man was for fellowship and not for man to depend on God for any further action from God; Genesis 3:8-9. Is your relationship with God one of fellowship, being satisfied with what He has already provided, or are you always needing Him to do more? Do you believe that God has already provided everything you will need in life, or is your life focused on what you do not have?

- **Principle Nine**

   God provided for Adam everything he needed to live; food, a home, work and responsibility, and material resources (including gold, bdellium or myrrh, and onyx stone—a precious stone that aids in development of emotional and physical strength, and stamina). Remarkably similar to the gifts that were given to Jesus at His birth. As a born-again Christian, in Christ Jesus, God has provided the same for me.

- *Principle Ten*

Genesis, chapter 2 provides more details of God's purpose, His provision, and His plans that were created in Genesis, chapter 1. The most significant part of His plan was that He rested and placed the responsibility for all that He had created into Adam's (mankind's) authority (Genesis 1:26-28). This is further confirmed in Genesis 2:19-20, when God brings every beast of the field and birds of the air to Adam for him to name.

The word "name" means to set its character, authority, bent, position, and comes from a root word that means purpose. By naming God's creation, Adam was charged with establishing their purpose. Adam used his words to establish the purpose and character of God's creation. Adam became a co-creator.

I can imagine the conversations that God and Adam had during this process. A Father and son spending time in deep conversation in the cool of the day. This principle is foundational in understanding God's plan for man and all that He had created. Do you spend time with your Heavenly Father, understanding His plan for the circumstances and issues of your life before you name it?

God's purpose for His offspring was for him to tend (to cultivate, to cause to grow) and to keep (to watch over, to guard, protect, have dominion over) all the creation of God...God never cancelled or changed that assignment. I was excited about what I was learning, but I knew that there had to be more. I did not know what, but this study was helping me understand more and more about my relationship with God. And you know that every good relationship grows and grows over time.

Two scriptures help me make the next step:
- Joshua 1:8 NLT, "Study this Book of Instruction continually. Meditate on it day and night so you will be sure to obey everything written in it. Only then will you prosper and succeed in all you do." From this verse I was challenged to meditate day and night on Genesis 1 and 2. I have been doing this since 2012.
- Romans 1:20 NLT, "For ever since the world was created, people have seen the earth and sky. Through everything God made, they can clearly see His invisible qualities-His eternal power and divine nature. So, they have no ex-

cuse for not knowing God." After meditating on this scripture, I was challenged to give detailed attention to the things that God had created: plants, trees, and animals. This curiosity led me to study various plants and animals and begin to understand God's heart in what He created. As an example, I watched a TV documentary on penguins. These birds would mate for a season, but when the baby penguin was born the parents would take turns finding food for their offspring. Each parent, on alternating days, would walk ten to twelve miles over frozen terrain, then swim another twelve to fifteen miles offshore to catch the food, and return to feed their offspring. I was overwhelmed with the care and concern that God put into these birds. Matthew 10:29 reminds me of God's attention to detail in all His creation.

With these scriptures echoing in my mind, I spent countless hours watching and observing nature and meditating on the scriptures, wanting to understand God's thought process. After all, I was His son, charged with the responsibility to care for His creation. I needed to understand His heartbeat.

Chapter Two ~

The Power of Love

First John 4:8 says that "...God is love": an amazingly simple but powerful statement.

What does this mean? How does understanding love help me understand what really took place in Genesis, chapters 1 and 2? Let us look at this in context.

First John 4:7-8 NLT, reads, "Dear friends, let us continue to love one another, for love comes from God. Anyone who loves is a child of God and knows God. But anyone who does not love does not know God, for God is love."

So, let us examine this in more detail. Love comes from God, and, in the context of Genesis 1 and 2, suggests that love can be a seed. It can leave a parent source and be planted, producing the fruit of love in another. It also says that if God is not present, then love cannot exist. Anyone who loves is a child of God; this confirms the parent-child relationship or the seed-fruit relationship. We, who walk in love, who produce the fruit of love, are God's offspring. This is awesome; it says that I am God's son and know God; that the more I walk in love the more I will know or understand God. By loving others, I will increase my knowledge of God.

This is exciting because I am responsible for my level of intimacy (close familiarity or friendship, closeness) with my Heavenly Father. But anyone who does not love does not know God—this is very clear as stated at the end of the passage, "But anyone who does not love, does not know God..." I can judge your knowledge of God by your love for others. Knowing the scriptures, while important, is not a criterion for knowing God, but loving others is. This verse of scripture says that the seed of love planted in the heart of man will produce the fruit of love for others, and that the absence of love is a clear indicator of the lack of knowledge of God. "God is love" tells me that the very essence of the Creator is love, and that the creation of the heavens and the earth is the fruit of His love. Everything that we see or perceive was created by love.

By understanding Principle Five (see Chapter 1), "God's system of perpetual reproduction," I come closer to understanding the plan and purpose of God's creation.

So, what is love and how does it work? If love has power, what can it accomplish? Well, the first evidence of its power is that you are reading this book. God's love for you was so powerful that it changed your life and caused you to desire a more intimate relationship with your Heavenly Father. And looking at who you were, all of us having an ugly sinful past, that was no small feat. In fact, the old you would have never thought and even wanted for this to occur. If God is love, then in Genesis, chapter 1, we can translate it to read "LOVE" created the heavens and the earth. That LOVE spoke and there was light, day and night, that there were the waters and dry land, grass and herbs that yield seed, trees that yield fruit whose seed is in itself, the beast of the earth and cattle and every creeping thing. That LOVE said, "I will reproduce Myself and have a son, Adam, or mankind." So, if God, who is LOVE, can produce all that we can see or perceive, then what can LOVE's offspring do? Or what has LOVE's offspring failed to do because he listened to another voice? Or what has LOVE's offspring failed to do because he did not know his identity, thinking "if I work hard, I'll get ahead," or "the color of my skin makes me think less of myself", or more of himself, or "I seem to be always subject to what others think of me," or whatever wrong thinking might be running my life.

In Genesis 3:11, LOVE asked His offspring, "Who told you that you were naked?" Or, "What would cause you to think that you were not perfect as I created you to be?" LOVE asked His offspring, "Why would you doubt My love? Why do you see yourself differently than who I created you to be?"

So, if God is LOVE, and LOVE created the

heavens and the earth and gave dominion over His creation to His offspring, then who or what is this LOVE all about? How does it work, what do I need to know to understand LOVE?

To help answer this question, let us look at a natural, or physical, example to help understand. Genesis 1:11 reads "...and the fruit tree that yields fruit according to its kind, whose seed is in itself."

These words created the apple tree, whose fruit is the apple, according to its kind, whose seed is in itself. God gave dominion of the apple tree to His offspring. His offspring has exercised this dominion to cultivate the apple tree, planting orchards and groves, harvesting its fruit, and using it to benefit mankind while perpetuating God's creation. This process has required planning, preparation, hard work, and an investment of time to be successful.

This illustrates the perpetual power of the seed-fruit relationship. So, if love is a seed, are we planning, preparing, working hard, and investing time to assure the success of its fruit, exercising our dominion? Is our knowledge of God growing and growing, so that the fruit of love flows from our lives, increasing more and more? Are we re-producing the essence of our Heavenly Father throughout the earth?

If the apple tree can become so prolific so as to occupy every corner of the earth, enriching and making full the lives of all who partake, are we cul-tivating the precious seed of love with the same energy and commitment? After all, love's potential is much greater than the apple tree.

God, who is LOVE, planted love in our hearts when we received Jesus Christ as Lord and Savior, calling us good ground for the procreation and development of love, so that our lives might produce much fruit.

LOVE is to the spiritual body, the Body of Christ, the same that blood is to the natural body. Blood flows through the natural body, bringing life. Life is in the blood, Leviticus 17:11. In the same way, LOVE flows through the spiritual body, bringing life. And because God is LOVE, when LOVE flows from one person to another, then God flows from one person to another, bringing life.

This life flows through the spiritual body in acts of intercession, kind deeds, encouraging words, acts of love, and numerous other ways when love that is birthed in the heart of a believer and then directed into the heart of another.

When the blood is cut off from the natural body, life is cut off.

As we love one another, we invite God into every conversation, every encounter, every moment of our lives. We perpetuate love or God throughout the earth.

Chapter Three ~

God's View of His Creation

How and why did God create the heavens and the earth?

Genesis, chapter 1, verse 1 reads, "In the beginning God created the heavens and the earth."

But let us stay focused on the how and why. We see in Chapter 1, Principles 1 and 2, that God spoke or used words to create physical/material matter. This is confirmed in Genesis, chapter 1, verses 3, 6, 9, 11, 14, 20, 24, and 26, when God said and saw everything that He said.

Then we see in Principle Five that "God set a system of perpetual reproduction for all life... every living thing has within it the ability to reproduce itself...this includes His Word." God's Word is life, John 5:24, 6:63. God's Word is seed with the ability to reproduce itself. And then in Genesis 8:22, God says, "While the earth remains, seedtime and harvest...shall not cease." Then in Genesis 1:26, God creates man in His image after His likeness, and then charges him, the man, to do the same: perpetual reproduction of the image and likeness of God. This suggests a motive, or the reason, or the "why God" for this creation.

God, the personification and essence of LOVE, had an offspring, Adam. And then placed Adam in the Garden of Eden (Earth) and charged him to reproduce himself throughout the earth. God used words to create life and charged His offspring to do the same. God's plan was that man would NEVER partake of the tree of the knowledge of good and evil; that he would live in constant fellowship with his Father; the Father always there providing everything necessary for him to carry out the plan and purpose for which he had been created.

Imagine a life in constant fellowship with your Heavenly Father, with Him revealing all the mysteries and wonders of His creation, and being in a state of receiving a continuous outpouring of God's love and goodness. This is the life that God planned for His offspring. The prophets of old saw this in a vision, calling it a "land of milk and honey."

Jesus told us that His reason for coming was that we "have life and have it more abundantly"; in abundance, to the full, until it overflows. It's an invitation to come back into the Garden.

Chapter Four ~

The Knowledge of Good and Evil

Genesis 2:17 NKJV reads, "...but of the tree of the knowledge of good and evil you shall not eat, for in the day that you eat of it you shall surely die." This was a warning by God that this knowledge of good and evil would disrupt Adam's/mankind's fellowship with God and the flow of life and love that their relationship provided. But Adam is tempted and partakes of the knowledge of good and evil and is separated from the intimate relationship he had with his Heavenly Father. And for thousands of years mankind remains in this state of separation until Jesus pays the price for Adam's sin with His shed blood and opens the door for restoration of mankind's relationship with God.

During these thousands of years, mankind's relationship with his Creator was to see Him as God, El-o-heem, Jehovah, Lord; the Supreme Divinity, Supreme Being, Deity, the One to be worshiped and served, and on and on. And all of this is true, but Jesus came to introduce God as our Heavenly Father and us as His children. The first, a relationship of the served and the servant; the latter, a relationship of father and son, or seed and harvest.

This knowledge of good and evil has also distorted man's identity; his understanding of who he is and for what purpose he existed. This is significate because where the purpose for a thing is not known, abuse is inevitable, acting out on a false perception of self, attempting to be who you are not, or doing what you were never designed to do; seeing life with a distorted view, never understanding truth, always making decisions with bad information. This state of being is captured in the word "ignorant": lacking knowledge or understanding, or being prone to arrive at false or mistaken conclusions; not being able to see clearly or to understand truth.

The new birth experience restores mankind to a place where he can choose not to accept the knowledge of good and evil. In the Old Covenant, we see God presenting this choice in Deuteronomy 30:19, "I call heaven and earth as witnesses today against you, that I have set before you life and death, blessing and cursing; therefore choose life..." Again, God is urging mankind to choose life.

Then in Proverbs 18:21, "Death and life are in the power of the tongue, and those who love it will eat its fruit." Here, God is reminding mankind that their words will publish their choice of abiding in His plan for their lives, or in death, the fruit that comes from the knowledge of good and evil. Then, in the New Covenant, John 10:10 echoes this choice.

God never wanted man to choose anything other than Him. This knowledge of good and evil is anything contrary to a loving full relationship with our Heavenly Father, embracing His will for our lives.

With the shed blood of Jesus and our accepting it as payment in full for our sinful state,

- We are redeemed and forgiven according to Ephesians 1:7.
- We are reconciled to God according to Second Corinthians 5:18.
- We have peace with God according to Romans 5:1.
- We have forgiveness of our sins according to Colossians 1:14.

And on and on, scripture after scripture, we see the precious blood of Jesus canceling, erasing, correcting, voiding the transgression of Adam, and restoring mankind by faith in Jesus to a life of fellowship with their Creator.

An example of ignoring this knowledge of good and evil occurred in my life. A year or so after my wife passed, I became overwhelmed with a spirit of loneliness. This loneliness was controlling my thoughts and daily activities. The Spirit of

God challenged me to begin a study of loneliness. First, I found this definition, that loneliness is an emotional response to isolation, that this is a normal human response when isolation puts pressure on one's emotions. But God called me His child, His supernatural creation. I then began studying what the Bible said about loneliness. I was led to the life of Jacob in Genesis 32:23-30, then Joseph in Genesis 43:3-31, Elijah in First Kings 19:3-14, Jeremiah in Jeremiah 15:15-21, Nehemiah in Nehemiah chapters 1 and 2, Paul in Second Timothy 4:6-18, and Jesus in Matthew 26:36-46.

I then came to understand that God used loneliness to help us focus and to understand the path to our destiny. It is a tool that He uses to separate us from average or common thinking. When I'm alone, Holy Spirit has me all to Himself and when I give Him my full attention, I become aware of the awesomeness of His Grace and I see myself in right relationship with my Heavenly Father, thinking as He created me to think.

In Christ Jesus, we are restored to God's plan for our lives that He outlined in Genesis, chapters 1 and 2, *Living in the Garden*. Our challenge now is choosing to not give attention to the knowledge of good and evil. Genesis, chapters 1 and 2 outlines God's plan.

First, God created the heavens and the earth, then He created vegetation, plants, herbs, and all trees. Then the birds, the fish, animals, and all creeping things. The Garden was prepared with everything that Adam would need.

Then God made sure that Adam was aware that He had also placed gold, bdellium, and onyx for his use.

Lastly, God put His creation in Adam's authority and blessed, or empowered, Adam to be successful.

So that when our life's focus is on the truth of God's Word rather than anything contrary to truth, the knowledge of good and evil, we use our God-given authority to promote life and health and wellbeing. But when we use our words, our creative force, to speak on this knowledge of good and evil, we give life to things that God wanted us to be dead to; in effect, bringing them to life, and using our authority to raise to life what God wanted to remain dead to us. It is our decision.

Chapter Five ~

Genesis 1 and 2, Personalized

Genesis, chapters 1 and 2, the Chris Harris Expanded Translation

Author's Note: Genesis, chapters 1 and 2 are the only passages of scripture that speak of man's relationship with God before sin infected the heart of man. It speaks of God's original plans and purpose for His creation before it was influenced by the "knowledge of good and evil." This expanded translation is how I have come to understand the beauty of God's plan revealed in the scriptures. According to James 4:8, God is LOVE so for a clearer understanding we will use LOVE as God's name.

The History of Creation

1 LOVE, prior to the existence of the heavens and the earth and time as we know it, LOVE considered within Himself a desire and the wisdom to create the heavens and the earth. **2** The earth was without form, and void; and darkness was on the face of the deep. And the Spirit of LOVE was hovering over the face of the waters.

3 Then LOVE said, "Let there be light"; and there was light. And LOVE saw the light, that it was good; and LOVE divided the light from the darkness. **5** LOVE called the light Day, and the darkness He called Night. So, the evening and the morning were the first phase of creation.

6 Then LOVE said, "Let there be a firmament in the midst of the waters, and let it divide the waters from the waters." **7** Thus LOVE made the firmament, and divided the waters which were under the firmament from the waters which were above the firmament; and it was so. **8** And LOVE called the firmament Heaven. So, the evening and the morning were the second phase of creation.

9 Then LOVE said, "Let the waters under the heavens be gathered together into one place, and let the dry land appear"; and it was so. **10** And LOVE called the dry land Earth, and the gathering together of the waters He called Seas. And LOVE saw that it was good.

11 Then LOVE said, "Let the earth bring forth grass, the herb that yields seed, and the fruit tree that yields fruit according to its kind, whose seed is in itself, on the earth"; and it was so. **12** And the earth brought forth grass, the herb that yields seed according to its kind, and the tree that yields fruit, whose seed is in itself according to its kind. And LOVE saw that it was good. **13** So the evening and the morning were the third phase of creation.

14 Then LOVE said, "Let there be lights in the firmament of the heavens to divide the day from the night; and let them be for signs and seasons, and for days and years (time as we know it); **15** and let them be for lights in the firmament of the heavens to give light on the earth"; and it was so. **16** Then LOVE made two great lights: the greater light to rule the day, and the lesser light to rule the night. He made the stars also. **17** LOVE set them in the firmament of the heavens to give light on the earth, **18** and to rule over the day and over the night, and to divide the light from the darkness, the beginning of time as we know it. And LOVE saw that it was good. **19** So the evening and the morning were the fourth phase of creation.

20 Then LOVE said, "Let the waters abound with an abundance of living creatures, and let birds fly above the earth across the face of the firmament of the heavens." **21** So LOVE created great sea creatures and every living thing that moves, with which the waters abound, according to their kind, and every winged bird according to its kind. And LOVE saw that it was good. **22** And LOVE blessed them, saying, "Be fruitful and mul-tiply, and fill the waters in the seas, and let birds multiply on the earth." **23** So the evening and the morning were the fifth phase of creation.

24 Then LOVE said, "Let the earth bring forth the living creature according to its kind: cattle and creeping thing and beast of the earth, each according to its kind"; and it was so. **25** And LOVE made the beast of the earth according to its kind, cattle according to its kind, and everything that creeps on the earth according to its kind. And LOVE saw that it was good.

26 Then LOVE said, "Let Us have a son, LOVE, Jr., an extension of who We are, (LOVE became a Father, signifying a nourisher, protector, upholder, the Source or Giver of whatever provides illumination, physical and spiritual) in Our image, according to Our likeness; let LOVE, Jr. have dominion, subjugate, reign, prevail, rule, overtake the fish of the sea, over the birds of the air, and over the cattle, over all the earth and over every creeping thing that creeps on the earth." **27** So LOVE created LOVE, Jr. in His own image; in the image of LOVE He created him; male and female He created them. **28** Then LOVE blessed LOVE, Jr., and LOVE said to them, "Be fruitful and multiply love; fill the earth with love and subdue it; use the fruit of love to exercise authority over the fish of the sea, over the birds of the air, and over every living thing that moves on the earth."

29 And LOVE said, "See, I have given LOVE, Jr. every herb that yields seed which is on the face of all the earth, and every tree whose fruit yields seed; to you it shall be for food. **30** Also, to every beast of the earth, to every bird of the air, and to everything that creeps on the earth, in which there is life, I have given every green herb for food"; and it was so. **31** Then LOVE saw and inspected (verified) everything that He had made, and indeed it was very good, complete, 16 requiring no further action from Him. Everything that LOVE, Jr. needed, LOVE had provided. So, the evening and the morning were the sixth phase of creation.

The Garden of Eden/Living in the Presence of LOVE
Chapter 2
1 Thus, the heavens and the earth, and all the host of them, were finished. **2** And on the seventh phase of creation, LOVE ended His work which He had done, and He rested from all His work which He had done. **3** Then LOVE blessed the seventh phase, this state of rest, and sanctified it, because in it He rested from all His work which God had created and made. LOVE said everything that He created was complete, capable of fulfilling every purpose that LOVE gave it, able to expand and grow and flourish and be beautiful.

4 This is the history of the heavens and the earth when they were created, when LOVE made the earth and the heavens, **5** before any plant of the field was in the earth and before any herb of the field had grown. For LOVE had not caused it to rain on the earth, and there was no man to till the ground; **6** but a mist went up from the earth and watered the whole face of the ground.

7 And LOVE formed a physical body for LOVE, Jr. of the dust of the ground, and breathed into his nostrils the breath of life; and LOVE, Jr. became a human being.

Life in God's Garden

8 LOVE planted a garden eastward in Eden, LOVE, Jr. new home, and there He put LOVE, Jr. whom He had formed. **9** And out of the ground LOVE made every tree grow that is pleasant to the sight and good for food. The tree of life was also in the midst of the garden, and the tree of the knowledge of good and evil.

10 Now a river went out of Eden to water the garden, and from there it parted and became four riverheads. **11** The name of the first is Pishon; it is the one which skirts the whole land of Havilah, where there is gold. **12** And the gold of that land is good. Bdellium (Bdellium is a fragrant resin from trees, myrrh, used for perfumes) and the onyx stone (onyx is a precious stone, a powerful protective stone that aids the development of emotional and physical strength and stamina) are there (the same gifts that were brought to Jesus, the second Adam, at His birth). **13** The name of the second river is Gihon; it is the one which goes around the whole land of Cush. **14** The name of the third river is Hiddekel; it is the one which goes toward the east of Assyria. The fourth river is the Euphrates.

15 Then LOVE took LOVE, Jr. and put him in the Garden of Eden to tend and keep it. **16** And LOVE instructed LOVE, Jr., saying, "Of every tree of the garden you may freely eat; **17** but of the tree of the knowledge of good and evil, (all thinking, actions, and words contrary to My word) you shall not eat, for in the day that you eat of it you shall surely be separated from My fellowship in your life, and the awesome wonderful care, protection, and provision that I have created for you will be hindered and interrupted."

18 And LOVE said, "It is not good that LOVE, Jr. should be alone, without another human being to love; I will make him a helper comparable to him." **19** Out of the ground LOVE formed every beast of the field and every bird of the air, and brought them to Adam to see what he would call them. And whatever Adam called each living creature, that was its name. **20** So Adam gave names to all cattle, to the birds of the air, and to every beast of the field, setting their character, their purpose, their bent. But for Adam there was not found a helper comparable to him.

21 And LOVE caused a deep sleep to fall on LOVE, Jr., and he slept; and LOVE took one of his ribs and closed up the flesh in its place. **22** Then the rib which LOVE had taken from LOVE, Jr. LOVE made into a woman, and LOVE brought her to the man.

23 And LOVE, Jr. said:
"This is now bone of my bones and flesh of my flesh; she shall be called Woman, because she was taken out of Man."

24 Therefore a man shall leave his father and mother and be joined to his wife, and they shall become one flesh.

25 And LOVE, Jr. was naked in the presence of LOVE, the man and his wife, and were not ashamed.

Chapter Six ~

Living in the Garden

Living in the Garden is God's plan for His off-spring, His Sons and Daughters. And yes, Adam got us off track, but thanks be to God, Jesus paid the price in full to invite us back into the Garden. Sin was the reason God put Adam/mankind out of the Garden, but the payment for sin by the blood of Jesus invited us back into the Garden. This invitation, however, requires that we accept what Jesus did for us as sufficient payment for all of our sin and iniquities. First, by receiving Jesus as Lord and Savior, and then by renewing our minds to God's plan and purpose for our existence.

God's plan was that we would never partake of the knowledge of good and evil. He was saying that this information, this knowledge does not promote life, but death. The blood of Jesus gives me the opportunity to make that decision for myself. As a result, I choose to live in the Garden as my Father intended. I choose to dismiss this knowledge of good and evil as not being beneficial to life. I choose to focus on God's abounding, endless, self-perpetuating love for me. The love that allows me

- To be His child, living in His care and provision.
- To see life as a child on Christmas morning, excited about what gifts are waiting for him; focused only on how much he is loved, filled with endless anticipation of what the Father has prepared for him.
- Living each day, each moment of each day looking for an outpouring of God's love.
- Living each day in constant fellowship with my Father, discovering His plans and purpose for my life.

Yes, there is evil in the world; it is a fact. But I choose to focus on the knowledge of God's truth, how much He loves me. To use my God-given authority, my words, the power in my tongue, to speak life and not death, and then witnessing the good that my words have created. And as my heart is filled with thanksgiving for God's wonderful gift of life, this light drowns out all darkness. And the brighter the light, the less the darkness. And this is the result of my choice: my deciding life over death.

Each day of my life, I decide to maintain a heart and words and thoughts of THANKSGIVING for all the wonderful creation that God, my Father, has placed before me, for the love that envelops my life, and for the Grace (the Person of Jesus) that gives me the victory. Each day I decide to set my EXPECTATION that God's love is always with me, giving me the advantage. Each day I decide to live a GENEROUS life, willing to give God's absolute best in every encounter and opportunity. Each day I decide to maintain FELLOWSHIP with family and friends. Each day I decide to maintain fellowship with Holy Spirit, attentive to His leading and instruction, maintaining the position of the PUPIL. This mindset, this daily success routine, has assisted me in staying focus on my Father's plan for my life.

Living in the Garden now becomes your decision, your choice to agree with God's plan for your lives; your decision to allow the LOVE from our Father to freely flow into your lives and then out into the lives of all with whom you come into contact. It is your decision to be LIGHT in the midst of darkness, no matter how dark the darkness. Interestingly, God never said a word about the darkness. He only spoke what He desired: LIGHT.

Living in the Garden requires us to not have an opinion (meaning a view or judgement about something, not necessarily based on fact or knowledge) on the things we see, but to just be LIGHT and SALT. Living in the Garden is a constant discovery of God's love for us and His attention to the details of our lives. It is watching and being attentive to what God is doing and refusing to give attention to anything else. It is releasing the responsibility for our lives and returning the responsibility to the Creator. After all, the creator of a thing has the sole responsibility for its purpose and whatever is needed for its success. Adam got things off track by his disobedience, but use your obedience and your trust in the Father's plan to put things back on track.

The Garden is no longer a physical place, but a spiritual place. It is a place where our relationship with our Heavenly Father is as He planned it. A relationship that invites His wisdom and counsel before we name or speak on the issues and circumstances of life. A place where we receive the fulness of His love and, as a result of His overwhelming goodness in our lives, we pour it out into the lives of others. Freely you have received; freely give. A land of milk and honey. A place where all of our emotional, spiritual, and physical needs have already been provided. A place where we are fulfilling the whole will of God for our lives...LIVING IN THE GARDEN.

P.S. Living in the Garden comes from what you KNOW. Just as you know your own name, that knowledge is a settled issue. It is not up for discussion or debate, it is an established truth, something that will never change based outside influence.

This book is a record of the transition that took place in my life; from hoping, from wanting, from believing that one day God's Word would be so, to knowing its truth as a certainty; a settled issue:

- That knowing we are the Father's creation,
- That He has wonderfully and skillfully made us.
- That everything needed for life and life more abundantly has already been established for us.
- That the Father has empowered us as His ambassador, His emissary, His power of attorney, to act in His place, as if we were Him.

This knowing positions us to just BE. To be light, to be salt, to be LOVE, Jr.

Biography

James N. "Chris" Harris, Jr.

Chris was born and grew up on the campus of Tuskegee University, Tuskegee, Alabama. He received his Bachelor of Architecture degree from Tuskegee University. Now a retired architect, his career began in the office of John Portman & Associates and then evolved to his own practice, Harris & Partners, Architects, for over 35 years. Notable local projects include the Hyatt Regency Atlanta Rehab, Atlanta City Hall Addition and Renovation, and the WCCI World Dome Sanctuary. He was Born Again at 38 years old and joined World Changers Church International (WCCI) in 1988, where he has remained. In 1989, he began WCCI's benevolence ministry (Ministry of Resources) and served as director for over 18 years. In 1992, he completed the WCCI School of Ministry and became a licensed minister. He is currently serving as the director of WCCI's Sexual Orientation Support Ministry, a position held for the last 12 plus years. He was married for 49 years to wife Saundra (deceased). They have two sons and four grandchildren.

Made in the USA
Columbia, SC
01 March 2021